TEENS SPEAK
GIRLS AGES 13 to 15

Sixty Original
Character Monologues

by Kristen Dabrowski

KIDS SPEAK SERIES

A Smith and Kraus Book

A Smith and Kraus Book
Published by Smith and Kraus, Inc.
177 Lyme Road, Hanover, NH 03755
www.smithkraus.com

© 2005 by Kristen Dabrowski
All rights reserved.

First Edition: March 2005
Manufactured in the United States of America
10 9 8 7 6 5 4 3 2 1

Cover and text design by Julia Gignoux, Freedom Hill Design

Library of Congress Cataloging-in-Publication
Dabrowski, Kristen.
Girls speak, ages 13–15 ; sixty character monologues / by Kristen Dabrowski.
—1st ed.
p. cm. — (Kids speak series)
ISBN 1-57525-412-3
1. Monologues—Juvenile literature. 2. Acting—Juvenile literature. I. Title: Girls
speak, ages thirteen to fifteen. II. Title: Girls speak, ages thirteen through fifteen.
III. Title. IV. Series.

PN2080.D335 2005
812'.6—dc22
2004059046

CONTENTS

To everyone with big dreams

Foreword

Hello, actors! Inside this book, you'll find sixty monologues for girls aged 13 to 15.

Here's how they are organized:

- There are six sections in the book. Each section includes ten monologues from the point of view of one character. Each character is described on her own introduction page.

- Each character was designed to have different experiences and views on the world. You'll see her in school, at home, with strangers, etc.

How to choose a monologue:

- You may want to begin by looking at the character descriptions. Choose a character most like you, or for a challenge, choose one that is quite different from yourself.

- Page through the monologues. There are dramatic, comic, and semicomic monologues in each section. Some characters are more comic or dramatic than others.

- Trust your instincts!

How to perform the monologues:

- Tell your story clearly.

- Know to whom you're speaking and imagine you are talking to just that one person. (Of course, if you're talking to more people, keep that in mind as well!)

- A new paragraph or *(Beat.)* means that there is a pause due to a subject change or another (imaginary) person speaking. Be sure that you know what the unseen person is saying.

- Play around with the monologue and try doing it a lot of different ways.

Have fun!

Kristen Dabrowski

POLLY JAMES

Polly is upbeat, energetic, and a little bit ditzy. She loves to talk and is very emotional, which often gets her in sticky situations. Polly's dad travels a lot and isn't home much. Her mom is very protective and a little old-fashioned. Polly is the youngest of four children.

BURN

Polly, comic
At home, talking to her mother.

Ow! Oh, my God! Ow ow ow! Mom? Mommy? Mom! *(Beat.)*
I hurt myself; I had to scream. Hey, are you listening?

What did I do? Does it matter? I burned my leg, Mom. I don't
want to go to school. I'm a freak.

OK, OK. Fine. I burned my leg ironing my pants. Well . . . I was
wearing my pants when I was ironing them!

I don't know what I was thinking! I was thinking, "Gee, my
pants are wrinkled and I'd better iron them since they look like
crap." I'm sorry for my *language*, Mom, but I'm injured. And,
by the way, crap is not a bad word. There are worse words,
you know. Like sh—

I wasn't going to say it. I know you'd go ballistic if I did. I can't
help it if these words exist. People say them. Not me. Please.
Give me a break.

Listen, can we get back to my horrible, disfiguring burn? It really hurts, Mommy!

THE DREAM

Polly, comic
At school, talking to her best friend.

I had a dream last night. What do you think it means? I was in a car with my mom driving. She was bossing me around like always . . . "Did you do your homework?" Blah blah blah. "Why can't you try harder?" Blah blah blah. Then she was gone, so no one is driving! Then, somehow, my brother's in the car. And I'm like, "What are we going to do, Ryan?" And he's like, "What? Everything's fine." "Everything's fine? Everything's fine? Can't you be helpful and tell me what to do?" The car is going, like, seventy-five miles per hour, Tracey. So, then he's gone and I'm alone in the car. I was thinking about trying to grab the wheel, but I couldn't decide. Suddenly, an exit comes up that curves around to the left. I think again about grabbing the wheel, but I'm afraid to. The car drives right off the road! It goes right off a cliff and I'm thinking, "What do I do? What do I do?" Then I realize I am going to *die* and I wake up. It was the scariest dream ever. What does it mean?

What do you mean I need to start making my own decisions? *(Beat.)* Is that really what you think I should do?

NOT SMOOTH

Polly, comic
At home, talking to her mother.

Hey, Mom, while you're at the store, would you pick up a razor for me? *(Beat.)* What for? Come on, you know what for—my hairy legs. *(Beat.)* What's that got to do with it? A person is old enough when they start to look more like a monkey and less like a girl. For me, that's now! *(Beat.)* What? Fourteen? Mom, it's *March*. I can't wear black tights or jeans until August eleventh! I have to look better before the warm weather!

I am not being a drama queen. I am being a girl—a hairy girl! For your information, Peggy Schibovich had a boy-girl party and didn't invite Sasquatch here because the boys all call me Gorilla-My-Dreams! *(Beat.)* I am *not* boy-crazy. Boys are jerks. But if I do change my mind, we'll have to move to a new town.

It's not funny! You don't care about me, do you? I hope that all your teeth fall out and when you go to the dentist he says that forty is too young for false teeth!

DRESS-CONSCIOUS

Polly, comic
At school, talking to classmates.

Thanks, Roger. *(Beat.)* You like it, too, Vince? Thanks! You guys are so nice. Hi, Bill. *(Beat.)* Gee, everyone likes this dress. What do you like about it? I'm just curious. I've never gotten so many compliments before in my life. Is it the color? I like the color. The pattern? *(Beat.)* No? Well, what is it about this dress? *(Beat.)* Well, I just want to know so I know what looks good on me. If you like my dress, you must know why.

Chantal, I'm talking to the boys here. OK, fine. What do you want? *(Beat.)* What? My dress is what? All the boys like it. There can't be something wrong with it. It is not too tight. I've been wearing this dress for years. *(Beat.)* Well, I don't know why I never got compliments on it before. I was trying to find out before you interrupted. Yes, I noticed only boys complimented me. So? *(Beat.)* It is not "sexy." Stop kidding me. Are you really, really serious, Chantal?

I am so embarrassed. What am I going to do? I'm stuck in this damn slutty dress all day now! Why didn't anyone tell me?

EXAMINATION

Polly, dramatic
At home, talking to her sister.

What's the point of tests? The teachers can tell if I get it or not.
I mean, I show up every day, looking confused and answering
all their questions wrong. Studying is stupid. And it doesn't help
that everyone else in this stupid family is a genius!

Even if I learn anything new in the next few hours, anything at
all, what's to say I won't forget it immediately? In fact, I'm sure
I will. What's the point! Who cares? What is it really going to
matter if I know when Napoleon made himself Emperor or how
a black hole is created? It doesn't matter! Plus, I'm a kid! This
pressure is too much! And it's only going to get worse. High
school, college—my God, it's endless! Why? Why! I don't need
to know any of this. I quit! I'm done. I'm never going back to
that hellhole. I swear!

TREADING WATER

Polly, dramatic
At school, talking to her best friend.

Know what? I actually don't like being a good swimmer. I know that sounds nuts, but it's true. It scares me a little. Everyone keeps saying, "You're the best in the school" and "We're all depending on you." That's scary. What if I stop being good? What if I lose? Plus, the pressure of wearing a bathing suit year round, having wet hair all the time, getting up early to practice—it's pretty horrible.

It's pointless to talk about, actually. My parents will never let me stop doing this. It's, like, the only thing that makes them proud of me. I'm not smart or really popular or amazingly pretty; I can swim. I don't know what's worse: Being really good at something and feeling pressured to succeed or being really talentless and feeling like you're a loser. They both stink. It's there anything in between? I'm never going to be happy. When will this suffering end, Tracey? When?

UNDERSTANDING

Polly, dramatic
At home, talking to her father.

Dad? Why do you say things like that? It really hurts my feelings. I *do* try. I *do* make an effort. This is my best.

Well, what am I supposed to do? It's not good enough, but it's my best. I don't know what you want from me. Can't you just accept that I'm stupid? I'm sorry you're so ashamed of me, your moronic daughter. Don't you think I feel bad as it is? You don't need to make me feel any worse. I go into school every day and I just wait for one of the teachers to make an ass out of me.

Ass is not a bad word! Dad, that's not the point anyway. I get humiliated daily. That is a punishment already. I don't need you making me feel guilty besides. But, listen, I've been thinking about it. And there's a lot of good things about me that you don't even notice.

For starters, except for you and Mom, people like me! Can't you even try to see the good things about me?

HELPING

Polly, semicomic
At Sunday school, talking to children.

Hey, kids? Kids! Excuse me. Hello! Kids!! OK. We're going to do an art project. *(Beat.)* You don't want to? What if I told you that you had to? *(Beat.)* Because I said so? *(Beat.)* I know I'm not your mother, and I'm actually pretty glad about that. I'm here for the same reason you're here, kiddies, and that's because my mom made me come. So can't we all just get along? *(Beat.)* No? What if I begged? Pleeeeeease, kids, please, can we just sit quietly and draw for the next hour? Look, look, I'm on my knees. Just do me this one favor. *(Beat.)* Hey! No hitting! Sit down! Stop yelling! You are the spawn of Satan, that's why your parents brought you here, isn't it? *(Beat.)* I don't care if you tell your mother what I said! Maybe it will get me out of this next week! In fact, everyone please go home and tell your parents that I am mean because I tried to make you act like human beings, you monstrous beasts!

I hate helping people!

SMOOTH

Polly, semicomic
At school, talking to a guy.

You're really funny. I mean it. There aren't so many funny people in the world, but you are one of them. I like talking to you. You're so easy to talk to. Lots of people don't really listen much . . . I know I talk a lot! Sorry!

So . . . I've seen you talking to Missy. Do you like her? *(Beat.)* Yeah, she's smart. Really smart. I think being smart is overrated. I mean, it's important not to be an imbecile, but a person just needs common sense. You know, look both ways when crossing the street, don't poke snakes with a stick . . .

You think I'm smart? You haven't been in any of my classes, have you? *(Beat.)* English. Yeah! You were in my English class. And you think I'm smart? Gosh, Brian, *you're* smart! You're the smartest guy I've ever met, I swear.

SHOPPING BAG

Polly, semicomic
At a convenience store, talking to a cashier.

Um, do you think maybe I could have a bag that's not see-through? *(Beat.)* You don't have one? Why not? It's important. Could I have, like, twelve bags or something? *(Beat.)* Mister, it was awkward enough bringing these items up to the counter. I'm actually really mad at my mom for making me do this. It's embarrassing, as you might imagine. Every horrible item is right here on the counter for you and the whole world to see: tampons, toilet paper, Pepto-Bismol . . . Quite honestly, I think this is a punishment. Do we really, desperately need Gas-X *right now* in addition to all these other items? I would seriously worry about a person's health if they had all these things wrong with them.

Very passive aggressive of my mom, isn't it? It's clearly psychological torture. I'll be telling psychiatrists about this in years to come. So, please, please, don't make this any worse. Is there any way in the whole universe you could supply me with some way not to have to walk back home, through my *whole* neighborhood, with these items on display?

Mister, I'm gonna love you forever.

JULIE WARREN

Julie is sweet, practical, and levelheaded, but she's going through a crisis. Her parents recently divorced. This former small-town girl now lives with her mother and little sister in a big city.

THE MOVE

Julie, dramatic
At home, talking to her mother.

Mom, can't we please move? I don't like it here. *(Beat.)* I don't care that you and Dad divorced. Figure it out how to get us back home! Isn't he supposed to give us money? You don't know what it's like. I'm, like, an alien in this neighborhood. No one looks like me here. I walk down the street and people hiss at me. The boys make kissing noises. It's creepy. *(Beat.)* They are not trying to get my attention! Well, they are, but they're trying to make me scared, Mom. They hate me. Everyone does. People scream, "Hey! Hey! I'm talking to you! Don't you ignore me!" It's scary! I hate it. We have to move. We have to! Have you noticed I still wear a hat and it's warm outside? That's because I'm trying to cover my hair. So I'm not so noticeable. I hate being ashamed of how I look. Why should I try to be invisible? I don't want to slouch and look at the ground all day long. This is too much. Please, Mom, we need to move.

PRACTICE MAKES . . .

Julie, semicomic
At a music lesson, talking to her piano teacher.

Maybe you haven't noticed, but I'm not good at this. I'm not putting myself down, it's factual. Really. I hate to practice. I am never going to be a musician. I've faced this. It's OK. I can live with that. If I'm being honest here, I hate practicing. I hate it. Actually, I don't do it. I know every week I come here and I say I practiced for hours, but I'm lying. I never practice. *(Beat.)* Don't say that. It does not show that I have natural talent. If I could just sit down and *play* something, something real, then maybe I'd enjoy it. But if I have to practice for years before I'm any good, I just don't want to do it.

Listen, could you speak to my mom about this? If *I* tell her, she'll think I'm lazy. And maybe I am a little. But I'm not cut out for this; I'm not exactly Beethoven.

Um, Mrs. McGraw, I just want you to know this has nothing to do with you. You're a great teacher and a really nice lady. Especially if you get me out of this!

THE ATTEMPT

Julie, comic
At home, talking to a friend.

Do I look any older? *(Beat.)* What? What do I have to do not to look ten? Look at me. Be objective. I put on my mom's makeup. I'm wearing your clothes. What more can I do? *(Beat.)* Try to look mean? OK, here it goes.

(Makes a mean face.)

How's this? *(Beat.)* No? What do you mean, "I look like I ate something sour"? This is the best I can do! *(Beat.)* I do not look innocent! I'm as hardened and streetwise as the next person. *(Beat.)* Walk? Why? Oh, OK. I can look tough.

(Walks in a tough, slouchy way.)

I do not look like I have scoliosis! I'm *slouching*. Oh, forget it! It's useless! I'm going to look like a baby forever. I'll be ninety, gumming my food in a rest home, and the nurses will tell me the elementary school is around the corner. I'm doomed!

WHEN IN PARIS

Julie, comic
In a Paris hotel room, talking to her mother.

Mom? I just went out on my own. I didn't go far. Just to the corner market. This place is amazing! It even smells different. Like perfume and cheese. The people all seem so sophisticated. I was trying to figure out why they all seem so chic—see? I'm using French!—but I can't quite put my finger on it. They just seem to know everything. So mysterious and cool. Maybe it's because I can't understand a word they say.

Anyhow, back to my story! I'm so proud of myself! I got a toothbrush and a bag of chestnuts. OK, I wanted apples and bread, but so what! I faced my fears and went out and talked to foreign French people. Sort of. I pointed and nodded while they talked. But still! I feel brave!

Oh. There's going to be some old French dude coming here looking for someone to pay him. I think I bought a cow, too. I'm not exactly clear.

INFESTATION

Julie, dramatic
At home, talking to her mother.

Mom. Get me out of here. I am completely freaked out! What do cockroaches look like? I think I just saw one. It was *huge* and black and crawly . . . God, this is the worst place in the world! I feel like they're crawling all over me. I think they're in my bed and my shoes. I can't stand it here!! I tried to kill it, but it was too fast. Mom, I don't think you are taking this seriously. Once these things lay eggs, which they probably already have, they're everywhere. We are going to have to live with these creepy things forever. Can't you hear them in the walls? Don't you itch? They're probably crawling on my face at night. This is a serious health hazard.

Isn't there any way you can get back with Dad so we can move home? This isn't right. I know you want a career, but does it have to be here? Here is disgusting. I can't live like this! I want a house, not a slimy, run-down apartment! Mom, I want to live with Dad.

STANDING UP

Julie, dramatic
At school, talking to a classmate.

This has got to stop. How long are you going to pick on me, just because of the way I look? You don't know me. You don't know anything about me. Why do you hate me so much? I never did anything to you. Can't we just call a truce?

I don't get you. You are so mean. But I'm not going to cry. Maybe I used to, but I was a different person when I first came to this school. I was scared. I admit it. You're scary. I never met anyone so bitchy in my life. *(Beat.)* Go ahead, call me names. I don't even care anymore. You hate me, everyone hates me. Fine! I'll just be alone. I don't need friends. Isn't that great? Well, I don't know about you, but I feel so much better now.

Go ahead. Beat me up. I don't care anymore. I don't care about anything.

TURNAROUND

Julie, semicomic
In school, talking to a classmate.

Frankie? Can I talk to you? Something really strange has happened. I don't know what to think. BJ apologized! *(Beat.)* I'm serious. Do you think it's for real? I feel like it's a trick.

I know I'm different than I used to be. I don't know if I like it. I feel angry all the time. I'm always ready for an attack. I liked not having a tough skin. I just want to be me, marshmallowy and nice.

BJ respects me now? Because I stood up to her? Nothing makes sense here. What's so admirable about being a tough bitch? I feel like the whole world's turned upside down. Whatever happened to being nice? What—-

Shut up, Frankie, I'm talking here! Jeez.

HOMECOMING

Julie, dramatic
At her father's house, talking to her father.

I am so happy to see you. I've missed you so much! Daddy, can I tell you a secret? Mom wouldn't want me to say this. We're a mess. Everything's really horrible since we left. I know you and Mom haven't been getting along, but can't you try to make things right? Get back together?

I know you're divorced. *(Beat.)* I *know* that Mom's the one who left. But I've been thinking a lot about this. You can be the bigger person, Dad. *(Beat.)* I don't know. I just heard that phrase somewhere. Anyhow, you and Mom loved each other before, right? That's why you got married and had kids, right? So, why can't you love each other again? *(Beat.)* Can't you even try?

Why not? How come no one's trying here but me? Can't you try for me, Dad? Just once? *(Beat.)* I think Mom misses you. I miss you, too. Please, Dad.

THE GAME

Julie, semicomic
At home, talking to her mother.

Yeah, I guess I'm glad to be back in the city. Not really. Not really at all. Except . . . Mom, Dad's a total mess. The house is horrible and he eats fast food all the time. He can't cook, Mom. He could die from starvation or get so fat he blows up. Do you want that to happen, Mom? To the father of your children?

Why is everyone so apathetic? Doesn't anyone care about anything? *(Beat.)* So what if I'm getting worked up. Aren't I allowed? Why do I have to be good and accept everything I'm told? *It's not fair.* It's selfish! I need to tell you this. I feel like I'm burning up inside. My life sucks, Mom. Everyone hates me at school and now you and Dad hate me, too. *(Beat.)* You *do* hate me or else you'd try to work this out.

Do you know the example you're setting for me later in life? Leave. Run away from your problems. That's what you did with Dad and now that's what I'm doomed to do. *(Beat.)* You can't stop me from watching Dr. Phil! I can do whatever I want! You're not the boss of me!

GET REAL

Julie, semicomic
At school, talking to a friend.

So. I go home, BJ, to my old neighborhood, and everyone is completely weird. I feel like I stepped into the Twilight Zone. I can't believe I lived there! They're *super* nice and friendly. "You have a nice day now!" They say things like that. I used to think that was real. How people really felt. No one really feels like that. Life is too crummy to think like that. Like those people at McDonald's really want you to have a nice day. They're probably mad you showed up and made them work. Until you came along, they were slacking off. Maybe they're in denial. Maybe if you just close your eyes to what's actually going on around you, the world seems like a really neato place.

It's weird. 'Cause my mom is, like, somewhere in-between worlds. She doesn't tell me all nice things like the world is a great place and everything's going to be OK. And she doesn't tell the truth either. She just, like, doesn't talk at all. And she hates it when I do. I think I feel sorry for her. BJ, my mom is pathetic. How screwed up is that?

ELLIS PORTER

Ellis believes in girl power. She is strong-willed and outspoken. Her activist parents are together and she has two younger siblings, Kevin and Mandy. Ellis has been brought up to be sensitive to injustice and to stand her ground.

LOSER

Ellis, comic
At school, talking to a friend.

Jess's brother is so weird. He's four years older than us, and he spent all afternoon yesterday telling us about his boring life. We're sitting around, hanging out. He comes in and starts talking about all the girls who like him. Not only that, but he starts telling us how they luuuuuv making out with him, 'cause he's such a great kisser. Oh, yeah, all the girls just want his bod. Come on! What a loser! First of all, he's hanging out with a bunch of kids four whole years younger than him. Second of all, he's a dork! Even *I* know that. No way is anyone making out with him. Not even if everyone else in the whole world died would any girl make out with him. He's a pizza face! Plus, why is he telling us this anyway? It would be like my mom sitting with us to tell us about her period or something!

I know it's disgusting. That's my whole point!

CRIMINAL

Ellis, comic
In the family store, talking to her father.

You know this is against the law, Dad. Illegal. I'm too young to work. I'm just stating a fact. You could go to jail. If I called up the police right now and said, "Hey, police. I'm here at my father's store—*working*. And I'm only *[add age here]*. That's right, officers. I'm underage. I tried to tell my dad, I tried to tell him that it was *wrong*, but he didn't listen. Please, oh please don't send him to jail *forever*. I think he'll learn his lesson in just a few years. By then maybe the calluses on my hands will be healed from all the floor mopping I was *forced* to do to help out at the store. That's right, officers, he's right here at the store now. You can come over anytime." Then they'll come arrest you, Dad. It will be so sad. I bet Mom and Mandy will cry. Mom will have to tell Mandy, "Sweetie, Daddy has to go to prison because he forced your sister into child labor. He's a very bad man, but we still love him. Maybe someday he'll come back after he gets out of jail." And we'll all cry and cry. Mom will have to work six jobs. Oh, it's going to be terrible, Dad. Tragic. Are you listening to me, Dad?

What do you mean, "Keep working?" You aren't listening to me at all! You never listen to me!

DONATION

Ellis, semicomic
At home, talking to her brother and mother.

I don't think it's fair that we have to get rid of some of our stuff from when we were kids. Poor people need *food*, not my old toys. It's my stuff, I should get to do what I want with it! Dad doesn't have a sentimental bone in his body. These things are important! They're memories, history. I remember how I used to cram as many stuffed animals as possible into my bed to ward off evil spirits. To throw them out . . . well, it's inhuman. Unfeeling. Maybe I want these things for my kids someday. Did that ever occur to him? It's like me and my feelings just aren't important to him.

I know this sound stupid, Kevin, but I don't see you throwing out your old model planes. What makes them more savable than my stuff? *(Beat.)* Everyone thinks their things are important, see? It isn't for someone else to judge. I'm going to take a stand. I don't care what anyone says. Nothing is going to go. I know Dad will be mad, but I believe in this cause. I will not back down! When I believe something, I *believe something*!

Mom, don't tell me you're on his side! It is so hard standing up for your rights. Now I know how Rosa Parks felt.

THE WAIT

Ellis, comic
At a friend's house, talking to her friend and her friend's father.

Hi! Happy birthday! Where is everybody? *(Beat.)* Oh. I'm the first one. Well, can I do anything for you? *(Beat.)* No? OK. I'll just sit. And wait. No, go get dressed. I'll just relax.

Mr. Bergman, is there anything I can do? *(Beat.)* OK. I'll just keeping sitting here. Oh! Mr. Bergman, how does Amy feel about, like, gardening? Between you and me, my mom made me buy her a herb garden, and I managed to convince them to let me get her a purse. But it's made of hemp, so it's not that pretty. My parents stink, quite frankly.

Hey, what time is it, Mr. Bergman? *(Beat.)* Just wondering. I thought I was here on time. Am I really early? I told my parents not to drop me off too early. *(Beat.)* Oh. How come no one else is on time? *(Beat.)* No, no, I don't need anything to drink. *(Beat.)* OK, you go light the grill. If you change your mind and want help, I'll be sitting here. Waiting. And sitting. Sitting and waiting. By myself. All alone . . .

I hate waiting!

PRIVACY

Ellis, semicomic
In the school locker room, talking to a friend.

Why can't we have private changing stalls? I mean, who wants to see other girls changing, besides boys? I just don't like being in my underwear in front of other people. Is that so weird? I think it's normal. It's cold, for starters. We all know there are certain people, I don't want to mention any names—Chantal—who love standing around in their bra and panties before and after gym class. Does that mean she is more normal than me? No. I think that is completely bizarre. Put some clothes on! That's what they're for. No one is impressed. I don't know who they're trying to impress. Yeah, you have boobs. Someone give her an award. *We all do.* Hello? We're *girls*. So get over yourself. Yours are not plated in gold or anything.

Kids are cruel, anyhow. Putting us in this kind of situation is like giving people fuel to make fun of you. If we didn't have to change so publicly, those mean people would have a lot less to go on. Think about it. Remember how mean they were about Ashley's underwear? You know and I know sometimes it's impossible to get your parents to buy the stuff you really want. Those girls wouldn't have known anything about anybody's underwear if we didn't have to all change together.

Who do you think I have to talk to about getting privacy around here?

HONESTY

Ellis, comic
At a friend's house, talking to a friend.

I have to tell you something. This could be unpleasant. I apologize in advance.

You snore. I'm sorry, but it's true. You may not know that because you're an only child, but you do, and it's loud. You kept everyone awake last night. You probably kept everyone awake on the whole block.

Yes, it is that bad. In fact, it's worse than I described it. There's like this long snotty inhale like this *(Demonstrates.)* and this blubbery exhale like this *(Demonstrates.)*. It's actually a lot like a cartoon character. I didn't know people actually made sounds like that. And it was two hundred times louder than I just did it then. I swear. I am not saying this to be mean. I just wonder if you ought to consult a physician or something. Maybe you have some sort of blockage up there.

No offense.

CULTURE CLASH

Ellis, dramatic
At home, talking to her parents.

I have to cover my legs and my head? Why? I'm an American. Why should I cover myself? Respect for what? Hold on a minute here. So I'm supposed to dress and act modest, but I'm also supposed to squat over a hole in the ground when I have to pee? And there's no toilet paper? Something does not connect here. We're calling this a vacation? Why can't we just go to Florida or California or something? How come it always has to be a different culture? One living in poverty, too. Haven't we helped enough poor people for a while? I know that sounds selfish and I'm lucky and all that, but I am so tired of building houses and cooking meals and gathering berries. Everyone else comes back from vacation with a golden tan, refreshed. I'm exhausted, jet lagged, my muscles ache, my hands are blistered . . . If I'm lucky, I'm the color of a deeply fried chicken from carrying filthy water back and forth from a stream all day. Maybe I'd appreciate it more if it wasn't what we *always* do. If it was a departure from the usual.

Do you have to be so literal? I know I'm fortunate to live in a free, wealthy country with shelter and food. But, I don't know, is it so awful to just be a little selfish some of the time? I'm a teenager. I think I'm supposed to think of myself. How else will I know who I am? One of the great things about being in America is that you get to choose who and how you are. Don't take that away from me!

DON'T SAVE THE WHALES!

Ellis, semicomic
At school, talking to a friend.

I've been thinking. I know, what a change. Anyhow, I was thinking, why do we want to save the whales and all those other animals? *(Beat.)* Whales *are* animals. They're mammals, not fish. Look it up. *Anyhow*, if I can finish, I was thinking that animals don't go out of their way to save us. OK, OK, there is the occasional tale of a dog saving a person from a burning building or wolves raising children in the woods (which I, personally, don't believe). But still, even if you believe that crap, you have to agree that kind of thing is rare. I bet if an animal had a choice between rescuing a person or another member of their species, they'd choose to save one of their kind. And we'd call it instinct! For any other creature in creation, it would be considered instinct to protect your own species before another. But we humans have to go out of our way to save animals? It's called *natural selection*. I think animals should just suck it up if they're going extinct, and we should spend our time saving *people*.

DEBATE

Ellis, comic
At school, talking to a classmate.

No, you shut up! Don't tell me what to do! You think just because you're a *guy* you can do and say anything you want. Well, surprise! You can't. Don't speak! I'm not done. You're a know-it-all, jerk. No one likes a know-it-all. Here's a suggestion: Stop assuming you're always right and interesting and intelligent. I don't know who gave you your excellent self-esteem, but they should be shot. If you're going to have opinions, you should at least research them, for God's sake.

I'm not done talking! You are so rude! Fine! Fine! Go ahead, try to defend yourself.

Interesting. For once! I think you're a big jerk. But OK. I'll go out with you. Boy, are you lucky!

ON

Ellis, comic
At a school assembly, talking to a teacher.

So, when are we starting? Five minutes? You said that five minutes ago. Time is moving so slowly! *(Beat.)* I'm not nervous. I've got my notes ready. I practiced my speech for hours last night. I know it. I know what I'm doing.

I am freaking out! Don't tell anyone. I want to appear cool and confident. Do you have any suggestions for me? And don't say to picture everyone naked because that would completely send me over the edge! Why would that help anyone? Who wants to picture the principal without his tie? Not me! That was a joke, by the way. See, I'm fine. I'm cracking jokes. My mind is sharp and alert. I am a born president of the class. And of the United States. This is step one. I hope by the time I'm older we can actually face the idea of a female president. Of course, my parents will constantly be coming by to tell me what to do. "Tax the rich," they'll tell me. "Send aid to China." God, I can hear the nagging already!

It's time already? Eeek!

GLORY HARRIS

Glory is accustomed to being around adults. She's often the teacher's pet and seeks to please others. Glory's mother died when she was little and she lives with her dad. She's an only child.

TEACHER'S PET

Glory, comic
At school, talking to her teacher and her friend.

Thank you, Mrs. Jarvie. My mom made this sweater before she died. Oh! Mrs. Jarvie? What about my homework? Don't you want to collect my homework? By the way, I love your haircut! *(Beat.)* Of course I noticed! I notice lots of things. Like Howard—when he lifts his desktop up, he's picking his nose or cheating on a test. Don't tell him I told you. But it hurts the rest of us, our grades and all. It's not fair. I'm studying really hard. *(Beat.)* Yes, I am a hard worker. My dad likes it when I get A's. Do you think I'll get an A on the science project? I worked really, really hard on it! *(Beat.)* Oh, goody! Thanks, Mrs. Jarvie!

Be quiet, Heather! I know and you know my dad did my project, but there's no reason Mrs. Jarvie has to know! So keep quiet!

REALLY SICK

Glory, comic
At home, talking to her father.

Dad. I still feel terrible. Why is staying home from school never as fun as it sounds? When you're not sick it sounds like such an excellent idea. Watch TV all day, eat everything in the house . . . But when you're actually sick . . . I threw up, like, a hundred times. I don't even know what happened on any shows. No one kissed on the soap opera. I thought they always kissed! It was bor-ing. As for eating, Dad, I have to apologize—I puked up a bag of Cheez Doodles in your bathroom. I'm sorry. I couldn't clean it up because I was too sick. I had to switch to the other bathroom. *(Beat.)* What was I doing in your room? Watching TV. Dad, pay attention! *(Beat.)* Don't yell at me! You can't! I'm sick. I feel like I'm dying. I need some sympathy.

Daddy, please make me some tea and toast? I feel better when you take care of me. And if I don't get better, I'll have to stay home tomorrow and who knows what might happen then. *(Beat.)* Thanks, Dad!

PUPPY LOVE

Glory, comic
At home, talking to her new pet and her father.

Oooo, you're so cute, little puppy! I'm going to call you Rupert. I'm so glad my dad finally bought you for me. You don't know what I had to do to get a puppy. I had to prove I was responsible for an entire year—doing chores, cleaning my room—it was horrible! But here you are, so it was all worth it.

I know he's my responsibility, Dad. No kidding! Yes, I'll walk him. Yes, I'll clean up after him. Of course I'll train him. Duh! You can stop talking now. I'm aware of what needs to be done!

Rupert, see how dumb people are. Dads are such a pain. But I won't be. I'll be so good to you. We're going to have so much fun going for walks and playing outside . . . What? You didn't, Rupert! Oh my God. My favorite shoes! Gross! Gross! How could you?

Nothing, Dad. Everything is fine.

You are going to pay for this, you little mutt. Shape up or you'll be sorry! You don't even want to know what life will be like if you keep pooping in my shoes!

OUT OF TOUCH

Glory, comic
At school, talking to her best friend.

Gretchen, can you come here a sec? This is kind of embarrassing. Can you keep a secret? Will you go to the music store with me? It's just that . . . I have no idea what I'm supposed to be listening to. My dad plays only classical and oldies. This is really embarrassing. See, I don't actually have my own stereo. I kind of have to listen to whatever my dad listens to. *(Beat.)* I know! It's cruel! So whenever people start talking about music I can't really participate. I don't know what anyone's talking about! I figure if I can buy some CDs, I've got two hours after school before my dad gets home from work.

Thanks, Gretch. Hey, can I ask one more favor? If you think the music thing is bad, you should hear about my TV situation. If I see one more episode of *Sabrina the Teenage Witch*, I'll kill myself!

THE PARTY

Glory, dramatic
At a friend's house, talking to a friend's mother.

No, thanks. No, really. I don't want any. *(Beat.)* OK, Mrs. Burns. I'll level with you. I really do want some cake. More than anything in the world, but I'm trying to lose weight.

Is it chocolate? Wait—Don't tell me. I *love* chocolate.

I've been doing this for three days. Three days of complete hell. I can't remember the last time I had cake. It's like someone upstairs is torturing me. I have absolutely no will power. Why should I have to deprive myself when no one else does? Do you know people are always looking at me to see what I eat? No one does that to you, right? It makes me completely paranoid. So I'm determined to look just like everyone else. I'm sick of being the fat girl.

Thanks, Mrs. Burns. I really appreciate your help. It's hard to talk about this with other kids.

THE DRESS

Glory, comic
At home, talking to her best friend.

I've been waiting to wear this dress forever, Gretchen! I bought it ages ago and I didn't ever think I'd fit into it. Every day after school I'd take this dress out of my closet and look at it. I love it. I thought if I looked at it every day, it would keep me from eating all the chips out of the cupboard. I haven't dared to try it on until today. I didn't want to get discouraged just in case it didn't fit.

I'm so scared! Cross your fingers! Oh, and have tissues nearby just in case I need them. Here's the moment of truth!

(Mimes stepping into a dress and pulling it up.)

It fits! It fits! It's too big! I can't wear it! It's too big! *(Beat.)* No, I'm not sad; this is the best day of my life! I don't care if I ever wear this dress. Let's go bathing-suit shopping! I know it's not summer, but I am hot, Gretchen! It's not fair for me to keep this bod to myself. You know what they say, "If you've got it, flaunt it"? Well, I've got it, baby. Let's go to the mall.

HORRIBLE

Glory, comic
At a friend's house, talking to her best friend.

Oh! Oh, my God! Sorry! Oh, my God!

(Walks away in shock.)

Gretchen. Gretchen. Gretchen. Come here. I am having a moment. Something horrific just happened. I think I am going to cry. I think I am going to die. I don't even think I can tell you! It's too horrible! I just saw something I shouldn't have seen. It's burned on my retina. Horrible. Oh, my God. I need hypnotherapy to get rid of this memory. Every time I try to not think about it—there it is! I'm going to try to erase it. *(Closes her eyes.)* *There it is!* This is horrible. I know I'm repeating myself! I can't help it! I've been traumatized!

OK, I'll tell you. Remember, you asked. OK. Ready? I just saw your brother. *Naked.* It was horrible. *(Beat.)* Yes! Naked! With all his . . . stuff . . . hanging out. *(Beat.)* Well, the bathroom door was unlocked and he was apparently getting out of the shower . . . I need to get out of here. I'm sorry. I can never, ever come back here. I'm going to go home and poke my eyes out now.

WINNER

Glory, comic
At a school assembly, talking to a classmate.

Yeah! I knew it would be me! Teresa, stop grabbing at my skirt! I have to get on the stage! Listen, I worked very hard for this award and I'm going to accept it! Now!

What? Stop. Let go! What? *(Beat.)* I . . . didn't win? But . . . They said my name? *(Beat.)* They . . . didn't? Are you sure?

Oh. Oh no. I just stood up in front of the entire school, cheering that I won an award that I did not win. This isn't happening. It's a dream. Did anyone notice? Maybe no one noticed. What if I pretend I had to go to the bathroom? That's what I'll do.

(Yelling.) Let go, Teresa! I have to go to the bathroom urgently! That is why I stood up in the middle of assembly! To go to the bathroom!

I'm sorry for yelling, Mr. Adriano, but I need to go to the bathroom urgently. *(Yelling.)* That is why I stood up in the middle of the assembly!

I am so clever *I* almost can't believe it.

CAUGHT

Glory, semicomic
In a store, talking to a security guard.

You don't understand! I was holding this for someone; it's not mine! And I certainly wouldn't try to steal it. It's a magazine, and, to be honest, I'm a little embarrassed even holding it. Look at it! It's called *Teen Dream*. Even the title is silly. And look inside! There are *stickers* of guys with their shirts off. They look completely stupid. I mean, what was this guy thinking? It looks like he's thinking, "I feel so manly when I'm topless."

Please! I'm telling the truth! *(Beat.)* I didn't leave the store with it. I was just standing here, minding my own business and some girl from my school handed it to me. I don't know who it was. I just know I've seen her before. *(Beat.)* No! You can't call my dad! Please, mister, please! Look, you can take the magazine back, stickers and all!

I have definitely learned my lesson. I will never *touch* a stupid magazine ever again!

BONDING

Glory, semicomic
At a concert, talking to her father.

Dad, it was so nice of you to bring me here. It'll be great to tell the kids at school about seeing this concert! I love the T-shirt, too. But . . . well . . . if people know I went to the concert with my *dad* . . . No, I'm not embarrassed by you. You're great. Other kids just don't do this kind of thing, that's all.

I don't know what they do. I think they go with other kids. *(Beat.)* I understand that you're trying to protect me. You're a great dad. I don't think most kids like their parents; I think they think I'm weird because we get along so well. But maybe you could just, I don't know, not look directly *at* me. We'll stand side by side but we'll pretend we don't know each other. OK?

I love you, Dad. Really. You're the best.

JESS BARTH

Jess is a rebel, a rule breaker. Jess lives with her parents and her older brother, Billy. Her parents fight a lot and her brother's recently gotten himself in trouble. As a result, Jess feel invisible and ignored. Her tough exterior covers up a sensitive interior. She's often a little touchy.

TEST

Jess, comic
At a doctor's office, talking to a doctor and her mother.

Is this really necessary? I'm not scared, but . . . OK, I am scared.
I don't want to do this. I don't see why it's necessary. I actually
feel fine now. I'm fine. That needle is so big. I have to go now.
Mom, don't make me do this! Stay away from me, all of you!
(Beat.) I *am* calm. I'm fine. That's what I keep trying to tell you!
I don't need my blood drawn. I'm sure it's just a passing thing
and I'll feel better if I lie down. At home! Not here. Take me
home, Mom. I don't have to do this. You can't make me!

Why are you so mean? I am not making a scene. Everyone can
not hear me! I am not yelling!!

Fine! Fine! Go ahead and jab me with that horrible needle. Test
my blood. I probably have cancer or something and then you'll
feel bad about being so mean to me. Go ahead. I'm ready. I'm
fine. Don't treat me like a baby. I'm fine. I'm—

(Faints.)

TALKING BACK

Jess, semicomic
At home, talking to her parents.

Why are you guys so uptight? So I said one little curse word. It's a very normal word to use. People use it on TV all the time. I've heard *you* use it, too.

You cannot wash my mouth out with soap! I'm an adult, practically. I can do whatever I want.

Don't start the "not under my roof" speech. I can't take it. I know it by heart. Give it a rest.

You can't doubly wash someone's mouth out with soap. Besides, you'd have to catch me first. I'm faster than you. I'm younger and I'm fitter. More fit. Whatever. *(Beat.)* I am not sassing you. You're too sensitive. This is just how I talk.

What if I don't change how I talk? Maybe you should just get used to it, fatty.

(Starts running away while last line is spoken.)

You'll have to catch me first!

FALL FROM GRACE

Jess, semicomic
At a school dance, talking to her best friend and a classmate.

No. It didn't hurt. Just a little twist of the ankle. Did Robert see me? Why do bad things always happen to me? I'm never wearing heels again. I think I sprained my ankle! So I have to hobble around like the Hunchback of Notre Dame at the school dance. This is just my luck. These things always happen to me. Nothing like this ever happens to Chantal Drake. She's so perfect. I hate her. Look, Robert is talking to her now. How come all the guys like her? She's not so pretty. She's hardly a supermodel. I do not get it. I work really hard to do everything right, and it just seems to come naturally to her. Life is so unfair. Oh my God, Joanna, Robert is coming this way! Look cool.

Oh, hi! I would love to dance! But . . . but . . . dancing is for dorks. I'm just gonna hang out. Wait! We could hang out together . . . Robert?

This is how our whole lives are going to be, right, Joanna? *(Beat.)* What do you mean "speak for yourself"! Wait! You can't go dance and leave me alone! Joanna?

UNFAIR

Jess, dramatic
At home, talking to her parents and her brother.

Billy! Why can't you ever shut your music off! I am trying to do my homework! Come on, I am begging you! I have a history report tomorrow!

Mom! Dad! Billy won't turn his music down and I am trying to do some work for school! Tell him to turn it down!

That's not quiet enough. This isn't fair. It's a school night and just because he's not in school because he's a *deadbeat loser* who failed out of college, I'm getting punished. *(Beat.)* How am I the mean one? I'm trying to be the good kid and do my work, make you proud, and I'm the bad guy. Oh, poor Billy. No one's nice to him. He's had it hard. Poor Billy did drugs in high school and became an addict. Boo-hoo. He was partying! Having fun! And it blew up in his face. Why am I supposed to feel sorry for him? Why am I supposed to tip-toe around him so *he* doesn't get upset?

Fine! I'm a terrible person. I'll go to my room and think about what I did—try to do my history report!

THE CEREMONY

Jess, comic
Babysitting, talking to a child.

Here lies Swishy. He was a good fish. He was a kind fish. He was an orange fish. We aren't exactly sure he was a he, but he had a very masculine vibe. For a fish. We will miss him. The way he swam was like poetry. The way he moved his fishy mouth in little O's like he was always surprised . . . Well, we loved that. Who wouldn't? He fought the good fight, our Swishy, surviving two whole months. That's like a hundred and fifty in goldfish years. Ah, Swishy. How we loved you.

Is that good enough, Gracie? I mean, Swishy was very important to me, too, but it's raining and very cold out here. He got a proper burial. Let's let him rest in peace.

OK. Say a few words. But try to be quick. I don't want you getting a cold. Your mom will be mad.

(Weepy.) Gracie, that was beautiful! Oh my God, I miss Swishy so much!

BUSTING A MOVE

Jess, dramatic
At home, talking to her father.

What do you mean "What am I doing?" I am doing the latest dance from a music video. The school dance is coming up so I have to practice some moves. *(Beat.)* Don't start. Everyone dances like this. *(Beat.)* What do you mean "it's obscene"? It's *nor-mal*. You just don't want me to have any friends. You want me to be a goody-two-shoes who wears little girl clothes and does whatever her mommy and daddy tell her. I'm growing up. You have to face it.

This is too how people dance! *(Beat.)* "Over your dead body"? Excuse me, but I think it's a bit extreme to have a death wish over a dance from a video. *(Beat.)* "Don't get smart with me"? That's what you'd say if I said a melodramatic comment like that to you. *(Beat.)* I will not go to my room; I didn't do anything wrong. *(Beat.)* You can't forbid me from going to the dance! OK! Fine, fine. I won't do *that* dance. Even if *everyone else* does. Are you happy now? *(Beat.)* No? I don't know what to do to please you. Honestly. I am trying here.

SECOND BEST

Jess, dramatic
At home, talking to her mother and father.

Why did he get more than me? I got clothes and he gets an iPod and a DVD player? Not fair. That costs way more. *(Beat.)* I know it's Christmas! It's a time for giving and you gave him more than me. You like him best, don't you? *(Beat.)* Don't start talking about the meaning of Christmas. We never even go to church. Christmas is a time for presents! And he got more! You've always given him more. Even Grandma always forgets my birthday. She never forgets Billy's! I'm always second best. I feel like I'm invisible. Why doesn't anyone ever think of me first? I sing really well. I may not get A's, but I get good grades compared to a lot of people. Don't agree with me! You're not listening. I'm sick of being the "other" one. Why don't you just admit you don't like me?

What's this? Another present? Oh. Uh. Thank you. Um, that other stuff I said? I still mean it, but I'm sorry to, you know, bring it up on Christmas.

TRASHY

Jess, semicomic
In the lunchroom at school, talking to her best friend.

You what? Threw it out? Not again. Well, what do you want me to do about it? *You* threw it out, not me. I don't want to stick my hands in the garbage looking for your cruddy retainer. Which, by the way, was *in your mouth* before. It's disgusting. And that enormous trash can is completely full of people's half-finished lunches. It's too much to ask.

I *know* we're best friends, but I don't wanna. Ask someone else. *(Beat.)* Your parents will not kill you if you don't find it. They won't. Like they would actually kill you. Give me a break. Start looking, Joanna! You're just going to have to pick through more garbage the longer you wait!

Don't beg. Please. Don't make me. Know what? *I'm* going to kill you if you lose your retainer ever again! I mean it, too! *(Beat.)* OK. You really owe me for this!

(Mimes putting hands in goopy, disgusting trash.)

UNDERESTIMATED

Jess, semicomic
At school, talking to a friend.

You're kidding, right? You actually want to see that movie? It's for kids, you know. Little kids. *(Beat.)* "Fun." You think that would be fun. Do you think it's fun when people point and laugh at you? *(Beat.)* No? Well, that's what they'll be doing if you go see that movie. Honestly, Julie, I don't get you sometimes. You set yourself up for ridicule.

Of course I have fun. *(Beat.)* I do not take myself too seriously. *You* take *yourself* too seriously. Maybe you should think a little bit more about what other people think of you. It might save you a lot of misery.

Now let's go hang out and look like we don't care about anything. *(Beat.)* You know, we'll stand around and look at other people. *(Beat.)* Of course it will be fun. Doesn't it *sound* fun?

BRUSH-OFF

Jess, comic
At home, talking to her mother.

This is a disaster. It's hopelessly stuck. I promised Joanna I'd study with her tonight! *(Beat.)* I *know* it doesn't matter if I look dumb in front of Joanna, but you never know who might be stopping by. I not saying anyone *would*, but you never know. *(Beat.)* Don't overreact, Mom. And let's pay attention to the problem here! Even if I acted like a complete idiot and went to Joanna's house like *this*, I still have to go to school tomorrow. It's not like I can go through life like this! Imagine it. Me graduating college with a brush sticking out of the back of my head, me going to work every day with a brush sticking out of the back of my head . . .

Oh, ha, ha, ha. Yeah. I'll just wear hats. You're *so* funny, Mom. How come you never became a comedian? *(Beat.)* I do *not* have an attitude! Am I the only person in the world with a grasp of reality? Sometimes I really think so.

CHANTAL DRAKE

Chantal is popular, especially with boys. She's rarely without a boyfriend and often has more than one guy vying for her attention. Chantal has one older sister and her parents are wealthy. She was raised mostly by her nanny and spends a lot of time alone. People often mistake Chantal for being older than she is because of her looks and her sophistication.

WEAKNESS

Chantal, comic
At a coffee shop, talking to her best friend and a potential boyfriend.

Where is he? He promised me he'd come by one o'clock and it is *three* o'clock now. I thought he liked me. He stood me up! No one stands me up! And, worst of all, I waited for him. Please don't tell anyone I actually waited two hours in the hopes that he might actually show up, bloodied and nearly dead. Because that would be the only excuse for not showing up! Death or near-death! Why did he pretend he liked me? Why did he ask me to meet him anyway? Is there a camera somewhere filming all this for some lame hidden-camera show? Next thing you know my pants will drop to my ankles, I'll fall down a flight of stairs, and my head will get dunked in a toilet. Boy, the studio audience is going to love this one. *(Beat.)* Yeah, yeah. There are other fish in the sea, but I wanted this one!

Oh, hi, Stephen. Well, since you asked, I am really . . . fine. How are you? Were you in a car wreck? *(Beat.)* No? I see. *(Beat.)* OK, you can buy me a hot chocolate to make up for it.

Wanda, I am so weak!

ADVICE

Chantal, semicomic
At school, talking to a friend.

You are such a baby. Going out with guys is no big deal. Don't freak out about it. If they kiss you or whatever, just go with it. Most of them don't know what they're doing either, believe me. I've been out with loads of guys. I started dating at, like, eleven. Ask me anything. I've been through it all. It's pretty much exactly like the movies. If you like them, just make sounds like you're eating a hot fudge sundae . . . mmmmmm. Like that. You know, if you're making out or if you want to pretend they're interesting when they're blabbing about cars or something. It's really no big deal. People make too big a deal out of the boygirl thing. We're young. Who cares if they *really* like you or you *really* like them? It's not like you're going to get married.

Get me my pink lip gloss out of my Hello Kitty bag?

Yeah, so, just smile and giggle and all that crap. You'll be bored with it before you know it; just like me.

THIN AIR

Chantal, comic
On a mountaintop, talking to her older sister.

Wow. This is high. Soooo high. I am at the top of the world. And I hate it! They never tell you how many people die from this. There are too many other things going on, global things, so the news never gets around to the hideous, bizarre skiing accidents. The air is really thin up here. I think I need at least four more lessons. And some hot chocolate at the lodge. I just don't think this is right for humans. If we were meant to ski, wouldn't we have really long, flat feet and poles for hands? Wouldn't we? Say yes! *(Beat.)* I knew it! This is all wrong.

That guy is so cute. When you wear goggles and puffy clothes and you still look good, that is saying something. He's looking over here! I can't stop hyperventilating! *(Closes eyes.)* I'm in a grassy field. A flat field. A flat, grassy field. A flat, grassy, freezing cold field, ten thousand feet in the air. *(Opens eyes.)* *Get me out of here!* You, there, cute boy! Save me!

INSTINCT

Chantal, dramatic
At a stadium, talking to a stranger.

Oh, excuse me. Um, your hand is . . . your hand is on my butt.
(Beat.) You know? *(Beat.)* Oh. Well, could you take it off now,
mister? *(Beat.)* Thanks for the compliment, I guess.

What are you doing?! Get your hands off of me! Wanda!
Wanda! Where are you? Stop it, mister! Help, someone! Get
away from me, pervert! Stop pulling at me. *(Beat.)* I am not
going anywhere with you. No! *(Beat.)* You're mad at me for
not letting you touch me? Give me a break! *(Beat.)* I am not a
prude. Let go of me! Why won't anyone help me?

How dare you call me a tease! You don't even know me. *(Beat.)*
I am *not* a slut. And I am not going anywhere with you. *Get
off of me!*

BATTLE LINES

Chantal, dramatic
At school, talking to a friend.

Didn't you hear me? I said I don't like that girl. You are either with me or against me. School is like a war, like survival of the fittest. Since we don't play dodgeball anymore, we have to find new ways to eliminate the weaker people and, at the same time, keep from being eliminated ourselves.

Yes, there are rules. Lots of rules! Here are some more, dingbat. You can't like who I like, otherwise I can't like you. However, you need to think who I like is cute. But not too cute. We have to pick on people who are weaker than us to keep our power. Especially people who could be potential threats in the future. But the most important rule, and the cornerstone of all rules, is that we have to stick together. Any decision we make, we have to make in unison. We decide together what people will wear, who people will like, who is cool and uncool. And I'm telling you, *that* girl is *not* cool. Period.

A FUTURE MOTHER

Chantal, comic
At a friend's house, talking to a friend in the next room.

Um, excuse me, Mimi? This baby is making loud whiny noises. Come and make it stop. *(Beat.)* I don't know what to do. She's not my sister. I've never been near a baby. Make it stop!

Well, there's, like, tears coming down her face and her face is all red and there's snot coming out of her nose. Listen, maybe she's really sick or dying or something! She's sort of gasping for breath.

Pick her up? Won't I break her neck or something? I'd rather not. Shouldn't you get out here and take care of *your* responsibility? *(Beat.)* Well, get off the phone! *(Beat.)* It is *not* important. You're just talking to Jeremy. I saw him wet his pants in the second grade, Mimi. He's not all that.

No, I will not sniff the kid's diaper! I would rather die! You get out here and take care of this mutant baby now, Mimi! *(Beat.)* Be quiet, you stupid baby!

UNDER THE INFLUENCE

Chantal, semicomic
At home, talking to her nanny.

Mariana, you wouldn't like me if you knew me. No one would.
The things I think inside . . . You've heard me say terrible things,
worse than anyone else. And that's just the tip of the iceberg.
You're the only person I even partly tell the truth to. Most of
the time, I pretend to like people just so they'll do things for
me. But inside, I'm thinking really mean things. Like now, I'm
really thinking about how your skirt makes you look fat and
cheap. No offense, Mariana. It's just an example.

It's my form of entertainment. It's the only thing that makes me
happy, thinking terrible things about other people.

I feel bad about the way I treat people, especially you. No one
cares about me but you. You're more like my mother than my
mother is. And what do I do? I call you a bitch, I tell you you're
fat. I hate myself, Mariana. I do. *(Beat.)* Yes, an ice cream would
make me feel better.

LOVE CONNECTION

Chantal, semicomic
At school, talking to a classmate.

Hey. Whatcha doing? *(Beat.)* You're really quiet, aren't you? *(Beat.)* How come you're all by yourself out here? *(Beat.)* I've been wanting to talk to you. I've noticed you looking at me. Do you like me maybe?

Excuse me, but this shirt is in fashion. It's not weird. Like you'd know, loser. When was the last time someone washed that *really excellent* shirt of yours? You sit here, pretending to be moody and cool, but you're just one step away from a lifetime of minimum wage and smelling like fast food.

So . . . You *do* like me. Just not my shirt. Fair enough. *(Beat.)* Yeah, I'd love to cut next period. Do you have a car?

TRIPPING

Chantal, semicomic
At home, talking to her father.

Daddy, please can I go with you this time? Mom gets to go this time, why not me? *(Beat.)* I'm not learning anything in school now. I'd learn a lot more traveling, don't you think? About other cultures. I'm sure there's culture to be learned on a cruise. *(Beat.)* Well, like about . . . trade. And . . . business. *(Beat.)* Well, yeah, shopping. There's nothing wrong with that. It helps the economy, right? *And* there are probably people on the cruise who've been to lots of other places and speak other languages . . .

Dad, can't you ever give me anything I want? *(Beat.)* I am not spoiled! How can I be spoiled? I never get anything I really, really want.

Oooo, Daddy, please, please, please, can I go? Please? I love you, Daddy. Don't you want me to be happy?

REINVENTION

Chantal, comic
On a beach, talking to a guy.

I'm an orphan, really. I ran away from home years ago. I'm kind of a free spirit, hippie type.

I'm . . . eighteen. I stowed away on a ship and came here. I . . . own a shop. Selling jewelry. Native jewelry. Umm . . . but I didn't need to work today. I have someone else minding my shop.

Sure, I'd love to show you around the island. What would you like to see? *(Beat.)* Well, I live really far away from here. You wouldn't want to go that far. We could go swimming at the hotel pool instead. I mean, since we're nearby. I . . . I know a secret way into the hotel area. Since I'm a native here and all. I can get you in. We could just put food and whatever on a tab. You could play your guitar.

That *is* the truth. You don't believe me? *(Beat.)* You can too be a hippie and eat at a five-star hotel. You don't know anything about anything.

THE AUTHOR

Kristen Dabrowski is an actress, writer, acting teacher, and director. She received her MFA from The Oxford School of Drama in Oxford, England. The actor's life has taken her all over the United States and England. Her other books, published by Smith and Kraus, include *111 Monologues for Middle School Actors Volume 1*, *The Ultimate Audition Book for Teens 3*, and *20 Ten-Minute Plays for Teens Volume 1*. Currently, she lives in the world's smallest apartment in New York City. You can contact the author at monologuemadness@yahoo.com.